D1192957

FAMOUS FAMILIES™

JULIO IGLESIAS
AND
ENRIQUE IGLESIAS

ACTON FIGUEROA

The Rosen Publishing Group, Inc., New York

For Steve Ferger

Published in 2005 by The Rosen Publishing Group, Inc.
29 East 21st Street, New York, NY 10010

Library of Congress Cataloging-in-Publication Data

Figueroa, Acton.
Julio Iglesias and Enrique Iglesias / Acton Figueroa.—1st ed.
  p. cm. — (Famous families)
Includes bibliographical references (p.   ), discography (p.   ), and index.
ISBN 1-4042-0260-9 (library binding)
1. Iglesias, Julio, 1943– —Juvenile literature. 2. Iglesias, Enrique, 1975– —
Juvenile literature. 3. Singers—United States—Biography—Juvenile literature.
I. Title. II. Series.
ML3930.I4F54 2005
782.42164'092'246—dc22

                                                                  2004015649

Manufactured in the United States of America

Contents

A MEETING OF THE SUPERSTARS

In August 2000, two members of one of the world's most successful musical families were playing in Las Vegas, Nevada. Las Vegas attracts some of the biggest names in music and comedy who perform for the millions of people who come to this desert oasis to play blackjack, baccarat, and the slot machines. Singers such as Elvis and Celine Dion have played here. On this particular night, however, these performers weren't playing together. In fact, they weren't even in very close contact. Julio and Enrique Iglesias—father and son and both musical superstars—were playing Las Vegas, but no one knew if they were even planning to see each other.

Julio, a star since competing in an international musical competition in 1970, was playing Caesar's Palace. He would be the last musician to perform in the Circus Maximus showroom. It was later torn down to make way for a bigger, more luxurious concert hall. Julio was fifty-seven at the time, and most of his fans were in

In 1999, Julio played several shows at Caesar's Palace in Las Vegas. While in town, he visited high school students and talked to them about his life and career. A natural performer, Julio is charming and at ease with any audience.

A young Julio Iglesias is shown here in 1979. Julio, a former soccer star turned crooner, was about to become Spain's best-selling singer and one of the most popular Latin singers in the world.

their forties or older. Some of them had been loyal to their favorite Latin singer for years. If the postings on his many Internet fan sites were any indication, these fans weren't troubled by the fact that their idol wasn't getting much airplay anymore.

Times had changed, and musical tastes had changed with them. Julio's romantic style of singing wasn't in vogue, but that didn't seem to matter to his fans. They sought him out wherever he performed, although he now played in much smaller halls than he did in the 1980s and 1990s.

This concert at Caesar's was typical of Julio's musical dates in the United States. This smaller venue suited Julio's laid-back style, and his fans certainly didn't mind that he was a lot closer to them than in the days when he sold out large arenas.

Farther down what's known as the Las Vegas "strip," Julio's son Enrique was also performing. Enrique was a relative newcomer to the music industry. His first album had been released five years earlier, but those years had been full ones for the latest Latin superstar to dominate the world's airwaves. He had an impressive track record: he'd sold millions of albums, won a Grammy, appeared in popular videos, and sold out his shows in enormous halls. This concert in Las Vegas was the first to be played in the newly reopened Aladdin concert hall—a flashy building designed to seat 7,000.

This was the situation: a famous father, who, for years, had been the leading Latin singer in the world, was playing a small, aging hall, while his superstar son was playing to a much larger crowd in the newest place in town. It is not known what Julio and Enrique thought about this ironic turn of events, as neither spoke to the press.

From the very beginning of Enrique's career, he had been competitive with his father. Enrique didn't even tell Julio that he planned to be a singer until he had signed

Enrique Iglesias is pictured here at the celebration to reopen Las Vegas's Aladdin Theatre for the Performing Arts in August 2000.

his first recording contract in 1994. Ultimately, this behavior isn't surprising. This is because both Julio and Enrique are fiercely determined individuals. They share the ability to identify a goal—in this case, international superstardom—and then work ceaselessly until they have achieved it. Neither man is willing to let anything stand in his way, no matter what the consequences might be.

CHAPTER 1

FROM AWKWARD KID TO SUPERSTAR

Julio's first taste of musical success came in 1968, when he won first place in Spain's Benidorm Song Contest. The contest is like an early version of *American Idol*: unknown singers/songwriters compete for the prize for best song. The other contestants were very talented, and no one expected Julio to win. He was just a skinny, pimply kid from Madrid. But he did win, and from that moment on, he worked day and night to perfect his singing and songwriting.

Julio's road to musical superstardom had actually started years before the 1968 contest, on September 23, 1943. Julio José Iglesias de la Cueva (or Julio Iglesias as his millions of fans would know him) was born on that day. Julio's father, Julio Senior, was a pediatrician, and his mother, Charo, was a housewife. Two years later, Julio's brother, Carlos, was born. The Iglesias family lived a comfortable life. Dr. Iglesias had a good job, Julio and his brother went to a good

Julio Iglesias has varied musical talents and interests. In this photograph from 1975, he is singing accompanied by classical instruments such as the organ and the violin.

school, and Mrs. Iglesias was able to hire people to help her with the housework and shopping.

Julio and his brother mostly got along well. People outside the family remember a certain amount of tension between the two because Carlos was considered to be better looking. Julio, with his skinny legs and pale face, didn't attract much attention from his classmates and neighbors. And not surprisingly, this bothered Julio. His mother tried to soothe his hurt feelings. A family friend remembers when, after neighbors complimented Carlos, Charo asked Julio's aunt to say something nice to him, too. Even at that young age, Julio was smart enough to know when someone was stretching the truth. When his aunt made a fuss over his looks, he asked her if his mother had told her to say that.

If Julio didn't always appreciate his mother's efforts to build him up, he loved and appreciated everything his father did for him. Julio Senior and Julio Junior developed a strong bond very early, one that continues to this day. Later, this loving, supportive relationship would be tested by a devastating event that would occur in young Julio's life, one that he almost didn't survive.

Thankfully, Julio's early awkward stage didn't last forever. Skinny and pimply he may have been, but in his teen years, Julio developed the charm and charisma that would make him an international sensation. He also grew to be a first-class athlete. Julio played soccer on his school team, and soon he was the star goalkeeper. He worked obsessively to perfect his skills. In fact, he worked just as hard as he would work years later to hone his singing skills. This dedication was the result of a love of the game. Even so, Julio must have enjoyed the crowds of schoolgirls who watched him practice every day.

A Brief Success Followed by Hard Times

Motivated by his dedication at age fifteen, Julio tried out for the Real Madrid soccer team. This, the equivalent of trying out for the New York Yankees, was a major event in young Julio's life. Nervous, excited, and determined, Julio performed well enough to earn a place as junior reserve goalkeeper. Soccer was the most popular sport in the country, and Julio became a hero in his neighborhood. For the next five years, he played for Real Madrid while continuing his studies. By age nineteen, he was studying law at the Colegio Mayor de San Pablo in Madrid. He had good friends, the admiration of his family and neighbors, and his future seemed bright.

However, things were about to change. On September 22, 1963, Julio and three friends went for a quick vacation in Majadahonda, Spain. Julio drove through the winding, mountainous roads in his brand-new Renault sports car. Returning to Madrid very early in the morning, Julio lost control of the steering wheel. The Renault slammed into the cement posts that stood between the road and the precipice, finally plunging over the side. When the dust cleared, Julio and his friends were amazed to find that they had suffered only minor injuries, although the car was totally destroyed. Julio's relief soon turned to despair. Days after the accident, he began to feel a terrible pain in his back. He couldn't sit up, he couldn't sleep, and worst of all, he couldn't play soccer.

Julio had always depended on his father for support and encouragement, and this difficult time was no exception. Julio Senior brought his son to every medical specialist in Madrid. They conducted test after test, but no one could find the source of his pain. Julio's condition became worse. Two months after the accident, he could

barely stand. Finally, he underwent a dangerous spinal exam. To his relief, the doctors finally had an answer. Julio had a tumor on his spine, which was possibly caused or aggravated by the impact of the car crash. Doctors quickly performed an eight-hour operation, which saved Julio's life. It also left him paralyzed from the waist down.

The Road to Recovery

With his hopes for a professional sports career destroyed, Julio was understandably upset. During this difficult time, he came to depend on his father more than ever. For the next two years, Dr. Iglesias worked with his son, slowly building strength in Julio's legs. After two years of intense physical therapy, Julio was able to crawl and then, after some time, walk with crutches. Eventually, he could stand, on his own two feet, though unsteadily. Even a young man with as much determination as Julio couldn't push his injured body all day. To fill the hours, he took up the guitar.

Julio often played and sang along to the radio with what his family described as a pleasant, unremarkable voice. When he announced to his parents that he would one day perform at the Benidorm Song Contest, his father was pleased to see a glimpse of his old spunk. At the time, it may have seemed like an unrealistic dream, but Julio's prediction was to come true in a few short years.

Fun Fact

Eladio Magdaleno, the male nurse who took care of Julio after his accident, gave Julio his first guitar to help him pass the time while recovering.

First Recording and First Success

In London, Julio made a demo recording of a song he had written, "La Vida Sigue Igual" (Life Goes on the Same), and sent it to several record companies. One company, Columbia Records, was interested in him and wanted Julio to make a new, more professional recording of the song. Even more exciting, from Julio's point of view, was the company's plan to enter him in the Benidorm Song Contest in Madrid—the one he had predicted he would enter two years before!

When Julio performed "La Vida Sigue Igual" at the contest in the summer of 1968, the crowd loved him. Not only did he receive the most applause, the judges were thrilled. In fact, he won. From that moment on, Julio never looked back. With the same determination he had brought to his soccer career and his physical therapy, he never stopped working to accomplish his goal of becoming an international superstar. And his work paid off. In 1970, he entered the Eurovision Song Contest with a new song, "Gwendolyne." Though Julio didn't win, he came close. People all over Europe began to think of him as the hot new singer from Spain. "Gwendolyne" was a massive hit in Europe and Latin America, and Julio toured constantly, traveling as far as Japan.

A Wife and Children

At this time, Julio met and fell in love with a young woman named Isabel Preysler Arrastia. Born in the Philippines, Isabel moved to Madrid in 1970 to stay with relatives. Julio and Isabel were married on January 20, 1971, and on September 3, 1971, their first child, a daughter named Chabeli, was born. Julio José followed on April 23, 1973, and on

Always a ladies' man, Dr. Julio Iglesias Puga (Julio's father) and his fiancée, Ronna, pose for the camera in 1994. Dr. Iglesias, a prominent Spanish physician, has always been a role model and source of strength and inspiration for his famous son.

May 18, 1975, Julio and Isabel's third and final child, Enrique, was born. During much of this time, Julio was traveling. He was touring Europe and Latin America, recording albums, and appearing on television shows. He even made a movie of his life.

All of his hard work was beginning to pay off. By 1973, he had sold more than 10 millions albums—all of them recorded in Spanish. Despite his time away from home, Julio tried to be a good father. His style of parenting included lengthy absences and doses of fatherly love delivered via long-distance telephone calls. He did the best he could as a husband and a father, but ultimately, it wasn't enough for Isabel. In 1978, Julio and Isabel separated, and in 1979, they were granted an annulment.

As Julio's marriage was failing, his career was gaining momentum. By 1981, he had sold more than 91 million albums. He was a star all over the world, with the exception of the United States. This was because Julio recorded his albums in Spanish, and Latin music had not yet caught on with U.S. record buyers. After Julio separated from Isabel, he moved to Miami, Florida.

By then, Julio had sold millions of records in almost every country of the world except the United States. He decided that if he was going to change that, he needed to actually live there. As he was settling into a giant new house, yet another dramatic turn of events changed the life of the Iglesias family.

On December 29, 1981, Julio's father, Dr. Iglesias, was leaving his office in Madrid when he was stopped by two men who told him they were filming a documentary about Julio. Always willing to help his son's career, Dr. Iglesias agreed to speak with them. Without warning, a car pulled up and the men tied up sixty-six-year-old Dr. Iglesias and threw him into the trunk of the car. The kidnappers kept Julio's father hostage for twenty days. During this time, Julio was forced to put his career on hold for the first time in more than twelve years.

In 1984, after Julio's father was kidnapped, Enrique, his brother, and his sister were sent to live in Miami with Julio in a luxurious mansion, pictured here. According to Enrique, "It [the move] was a terrible culture shock . . . I used to cry every single day."

Unable to think of anything but his father, Julio worked with the Spanish police and antiterrorist groups in an effort to locate his dad. When Dr. Iglesias was found, exhausted but otherwise fine, Julio

Fun Fact

Julio is not only a great singer, he's also a smart businessman. In 1989, he launched a perfume, called Only, and in 1997, he began selling his own collection of wines from France, Spain, and California.

made a decision that was to have a profound effect on both his family and the music industry. He brought his three children (who had been living with their mother in Madrid) to Miami to live with him. Julio felt that his new Miami home, built on an island accessible by a guarded causeway (a raised road that connects an island to the mainland), would be the safest place for his children.

Finally—A Star in the United States

Ironically, immediately after this dramatic and frightening event, Julio experienced his most important career success to date—he finally cracked the American market. Beginning in 1983, with the help of a new talent agency, Julio began appearing on popular American television programs like *The Tonight Show* and *20/20*. At that time, he also recorded a duet, "To All the Girls I've Loved Before," with country star Willie Nelson. The song eventually became something of a classic. While the combination of a gritty country singer and the smooth Latin lover might seem odd, it was an instant hit with the public.

Julio's next album, *1100 Bel Air Place* (which was recorded in English in 1984) was an enormous success both in the United States and the rest of the world. Success after success followed the man who, in 1963, thought he might never walk again, let alone become an international superstar.

In 1983, Julio *(left)* was a guest on Johnny Carson's *Tonight Show*. At that time, he was just beginning to get popular in the United States and was on tour promoting his latest album, *Amor, Amor, Amor*, which he recorded in English.

In fact, in 1983, Julio was awarded the Diamond Record Award from the *Guinness Book of World Records* for having sold more than 100 million albums in six different languages. This made him the most successful recording artist of his time. In 1985, he was awarded a star on Hollywood's Walk of Fame. Meanwhile, he continued to record albums that sold millions all over the world, and his concerts constantly sold out.

Twenty years later, this success continues. Since 1983, Julio has performed more than 600 shows in Las Vegas. He still records albums, although he hasn't recorded in English since 1994. While he is no longer known as the hot new Latin singer, Julio has active fan clubs all over the world. Do a Web search on his name and you'll find many fan sites devoted to the first Latin singer to achieve worldwide fame.

From his first public performance at a small pub in London to his success at the Benidorm Song Contest in Madrid to the thousands of concerts he's performed since, Julio has maintained his stardom the same way he regained the use of his paralyzed legs—through determination and hard work.

Pictured here, Julio Iglesias *(far left)* is joined by United States president Ronald Reagan and the first lady, Nancy Reagan. They are singing Christmas carols on the 1983 *Christmas in Washington* entertainment show. Singer Andy Williams also appeared on the show.

CHAPTER 2

ENRIQUE: SON OF A SUPERSTAR

Enrique Iglesias may have been born to one of the most popular singers of all time, but in many respects, his early life was just like that of any other kid. From the time he was old enough to follow his siblings around, his older sister, Chabeli, and older brother, Julio José, teased and protected him. The three siblings were close. They truly liked each other, but also there weren't many kids their age in the neighborhood. The Iglesias family was different. For one thing, most fathers weren't international superstars. As well, other families didn't need to worry about the press or keep bodyguards on staff to protect them from overeager fans and potential kidnappers. And what was perhaps worst of all for Chabeli, Julio José, and Enrique was that—unlike most kids, even those with divorced parents—they saw their dad only once in a while. At that time, Julio was always on tour or in the studio—often in another country. When the Iglesias children did see their father, he was either exhausted or planning his next album.

Julio, his daughter, Chabeli, and his sons, Enrique and Julio José. are seen in this 1998 photograph, just three years after they came to live with him in Florida. Chabeli has appeared on several TV shows and has hosted her own program. She is now a journalist who lives and works in Washington, D.C. In 1999, she was severely injured in a terrible car accident, and, like her father many years before, she miraculously recovered.

A New Home

After Julio and Isabel separated in 1978, Julio moved out of their house in Madrid and eventually moved to Miami. The family had begun to adjust to the new situation when the kidnapping of Dr. Iglesias, Enrique's grandfather, brought about another change. In 1984, the three kids were sent to live with their father in Miami. For nine-year-old Enrique, these were hard times. Despite the more relaxed atmosphere in Miami, Enrique missed his mother. As Enrique would later tell a writer in *Rolling Stone* magazine, "Once I got here, I missed all my friends from Spain, my mother, and it was pretty hard. I used to cry every single day."

As tough as it was to adjust to life in a new country, there were some bright spots. Meeting Michael Jackson was one of them. This was around the time of Jackson's enormous success. His album *Thriller* (1982), with songs like "Beat It" and "Billie Jean," is still the second best-selling record in terms of sales in the United States. Having him as a houseguest made Enrique the envy of all his friends. The beach-oriented lifestyle in Miami also appealed to Enrique. As a result, he became a skillful windsurfer.

When Enrique moved in with his father, a member of the Iglesias household staff became a vital part of his world. After his mother, his nanny Elvira Olivares was the most important woman in Enrique's life. With his father away and his mother in Madrid, Enrique came to

Enrique practices Catholicism, as do most of the people living in Spain. He is shown here on the night before his first communion, which took place in 1984. Enrique is sitting between his parents, Julio and Isabel, who had divorced four years earlier.

depend on Olivares for the support and love one usually gets from one's parents. This strong bond continues. In fact, without Olivares's support, Enrique might never have become the musical superstar he is today.

American Childhood

Enrique settled into life in Miami. He went to school, he swam in the ocean, he watched movies, and he played with his brother and sister.

Like many creative kids, Enrique tended to be a mischief-maker in grade school. His restless energy sometimes got him into trouble. For example, once he was suspended (according to local gossip) for putting a lizard on his third-grade teacher's back.

Nonetheless, Enrique was a smart and responsible kid, and by the time he reached junior high, he had settled down. No one from his junior high or high school years remembers him being a trouble-maker. In fact, Enrique didn't make much of an impression on his classmates at all. Although he has grown up to be a handsome man, in his early teens, Enrique was quite short. Also, he thought he was so ugly that no one would date him. This upset young Enrique (as it would anyone), and he often wrote his feelings down in a notebook. The words in this notebook soon took shape as song lyrics, which Enrique would sing to himself when he was alone. Eventually, out of teenage despair, a singing career was born.

A Growing Interest in Music

By the time he was fifteen, Enrique, although still a student at Gulliver Preparatory School in Miami, began to think seriously about a career in music. However, Enrique kept this dream to himself. He was still unsure of his own abilities, and being secretive seemed the best way to ensure that his dreams would come true.

One day, when he was returning home from school, Enrique stopped at a restaurant where two local musicians were performing. After their set, Enrique told them how much he enjoyed their music. The two men, Mario Martinelli and Roberto Morales, invited

Enrique to their recording studio so they could hear him sing the songs he had composed. They were pleasantly surprised by his talent, and soon, Enrique was racing to their studio every day after school.

For the next several years, Enrique continued to keep the musical part of his life a secret. He graduated from high school and enrolled at the University of Miami, where he studied business administration. Though he liked college life, his desire to be a singer was still strong. Because of this, after his second year, he decided to leave school to try to make it as a singer. Knowing that he needed a manager, he contacted one of his father's former associates, Fernan Martinez, who came to hear his songs.

Fun Fact

Enrique loves to read; Ernest Hemingway's books are his favorites. However, due to his busy schedule, his usual daily reading consists of magazines. He says reading them helps keep him up-to-date.

As soon as Martinez heard Enrique sing, he knew that this young guy had what it takes to be a huge success. Martinez described his plans to make a demo record and send it to all of the big record labels. Enrique listened carefully and agreed to everything, with one exception. He would not record the demo under his own name. To avoid any preferential treatment because of his father's fame, he would be known as Enrique Martinez. His new manager listened in disbelief. He tried to convince Enrique that it was crazy not to use every possible advantage one had in the ruthless music industry. However, Enrique wouldn't budge.

Fun Fact

Although his fans don't complain, Enrique considers himself very clumsy—he has often fallen during his performances.

A Big Secret

Before he could cut his demo record, Enrique had one more problem to deal with. Where was he going to get the money to make it? Studio time and musicians cost money, money that Enrique—for all the wealth of his surroundings—just didn't have. He refused to ask his parents for any help, as that would have given away his secret. His beloved nanny, Elvira Olivares, came to the rescue. She loaned Enrique the $5,000 that was needed for the demo record.

When the demo was finished, Fernan Martinez sent the recording to every major studio, along with a letter describing this mysterious new artist, Enrique Martinez. One by one, the rejection letters came back. Before Enrique lost all hope, a small company in California—Fonovisa—signed him to a three-record deal. Enrique had decided that, despite his love of American pop music, his first records should be recorded in Spanish. He also decided that, since Fonovisa had signed him on the strength of his voice alone, he was now willing to be known as Enrique Iglesias. Accordingly, in 1995, he released his first album, *Enrique Iglesias*. Music lovers all over the world were curious about what Enrique's father would think about his son's new career. Julio remained silent.

An Instant Success

The music industry is a tough business. Talent alone isn't any guarantee that a singer will be successful. Good looks, a well-known family name, and charisma can help an artist, but they don't guarantee success. When Enrique's first album was an immediate hit and went on to sell a total of 5.8 million copies, even his biggest supporters were amazed.

Enrique was poised to have a terrific career. However, not everyone was impressed. As Enrique told the *London Sunday Times* in 2002, "When I sold a million copies, [my father] would say 'You know, you're not going to pass a million copies—that's impossible,' . . . and then I would end up selling two million or three million or four million. Then he'd say, 'Oh yeah, you sold that many, but you're never going to win a Grammy.'"

In this 1997 photograph, Enrique shows off his Grammy Award for Best Latin Pop Performance, which he was given for his album *Enrique Iglesias*.

Eventually, Enrique proved his father wrong and won a Grammy for Best Latin Pop Performance in 1997. As Julio's own career was slowing down, it must have been hard for him to see his youngest son creating the same kind of excitement he had stirred up himself twenty years before. As a result, relations between father and son became quite strained.

Enrique had so much to do that he didn't waste any time worrying about what his father thought of his career. Enrique's second album, *Vivir* (To Live), which was released in 1997, sold more than 5 million

At the 2002 MTV Video Music Awards, Jimmy Fallon, known for his work as a comedic actor on the long-running TV show *Saturday Night Live*, performed his famous Enrique Iglesias impersonation.

copies and earned him a platinum record. His third album, *Cosas del Amor* (Love's Things), was another amazing success. Because Enrique's first three albums had all been recorded in Spanish, when it came time to go into the studio for his fourth album, he was ready to try something different.

He recorded a single, "Bailamos" (We Dance), which was sung in English. At that time, movie star and rapper Will Smith was looking for music for the soundtrack of his new movie *Wild Wild West*. Smith asked Enrique if he could use the song. Enrique agreed, and when the movie was released in 1999, he had his first hit single in English.

Success in English

On the strength of that hit and his three previous smash albums, Enrique signed the biggest deal of his life: a $44 million contract with Universal/Interscope Records for three albums in Spanish and three albums in English. Once again, Enrique rose to the challenge. In 1999, his first album sung entirely in English, *Enrique*, sold 5 million copies worldwide and included the hit "Could I Have This Kiss Forever?" with Whitney Houston.

It seemed as though everything Enrique touched turned to gold—or platinum. By 2000, he had sold 17 million albums, performed at the Super Bowl, and won a Grammy. He toured the world in a private jet and performed in front of thousands of screaming fans.

The newspapers covered his personal life almost as carefully as they followed his career. Even his famous facial mole (the subject of some memorable skits on *Saturday Night Live*) is of interest to his fans. In the summer of 2003, Enrique had it removed. On a recent U.S. television program he told an interviewer, "I

Like his father, Enrique has toured around the world. Pictured here during the 7 tour in 2004, Enrique charms the press in India, where he performed in Bombay and in Bangalore.

went to the doctor one day and he said, 'I can have it removed in five minutes,' and I'm like, 'Really?'" His fans don't seem to mind that there is a little bit less of Enrique to love.

 **CHAPTER 3**

THE IGLESIAS FAMILY

Life in the Iglesias household wasn't like that of the average family. First of all, by the time Enrique, Julio José, and Chabeli moved in with their father, Julio was already an international superstar. Besides their nanny Elvira Olivares, the children relied on Julio's girlfriend at the time (Virginia Sipi) for companionship and guidance. It wasn't until the children became older that they began to assert themselves.

Chabeli, the oldest, was the first to leave home. She began working as a model in Spain. At the age of twenty-one, she was already married and divorced. Since then, she has worked as a television talk show host for Univision, a Spanish language network based in Miami. Julio José is a singer with a pleasant voice, although he has not had the success his father and brother enjoy.

It seems like all of the family members have followed Dr. Iglesias's example. Dr. Iglesias was an extremely successful doctor in Madrid and worked

In this 1994 photograph, Enrique's adoration for his mother, Isabel Preysler, is clearly visible. Isabel and her family—who knew show-business legends such as Tyrone Power—moved to Spain in the 1970s.

In 2002, a concert was held in New York City's Times Square to kick off that year's National Football League (NFL) season. Enrique performed along with other musicians such as Jon Bon Jovi, Alicia Keys, Eve, and the cast of *Rent*, a popular Broadway musical.

long hours well into his sixties. He taught his sons that hard work and persistent effort pay off.

Julio learned this lesson well and has passed it on to Enrique. Both father and son are perfectionists when it comes to their music. Julio has a reputation for working long hours in the studio to make sure his songs are exactly the way he feels they should be. He wants his fans to hear his best work.

Julio's popularity, which he has enjoyed for four decades, indicates that his fans like what he's doing. And Enrique appears to have a real devotion to his fans. For example, when there was a speaker malfunction at a concert in Toronto in 2003, many fans couldn't hear very well. Enrique insisted on returning to

Fun Fact

Enrique's face has appeared on more than 250 magazine covers, and he has recorded more than 190 television programs in twenty-three countries.

Toronto later that year to give another performance for anyone who had attended the first concert. In fact, Enrique offered free tickets to 2,500 fans. Both Julio and Enrique work very hard to give their fans a good performance, whether on a CD or in concert, and that kind of respect for the fans is part of what makes them both superstars.

CHAPTER 4

THEIR LATEST PROJECTS

In the years since Julio and Enrique played their separate concerts in Las Vegas, both have continued to work steadily—performing and producing music for their fans. Julio produced several albums, all of them in Spanish. (His last album in English, *Crazy*, was released in 1994.) He continues to be a hard-working perfectionist in the studio, often working on two albums at the same time, determined to make them as close to perfect as he can.

To make his difficult schedule easier for himself and his family, Julio has built recording studios in his homes, including one at his beach house in the Caribbean. This allows him to spend time with his wife, Miranda, and their four children, all born since 1997. It also allows Julio to see more of his father, who, at eighty-seven years of age, fathered a child with his forty-year-old wife. (This means that Enrique has an uncle who is twenty-eight years younger than he is.)

Julio enjoys himself during a 2003 photo shoot in Madrid, during which he presented his latest album, *Divorcio*. *Divorcio*, Julio's seventy-sixth and perhaps most personal song album, went double platinum in Spain on the first day it was released.

In April 2003, at the age of sixty, Julio released *Frontieras* (Frontiers), with songs sung in five languages. He followed this up with *Divorcio*, which he released in 2003. Despite the album's title, which is the Spanish word for "divorce," Julio and Miranda are still happily married.

The Never-Ending Tour

Julio continues to tour—both close to home and as far away as Asia. As always, he continues to push himself, singing songs in many different languages. "Sometimes I sing in Chinese and Japanese, but these [songs] are a little more difficult," he told the *Las Vegas Review-Journal* in 2003. "I have to, you know? I play Asia two months of the year." This dedicated and driven performer is glad to have a home on the stages of the world. In the same article, he said, "For the last four or five years, I've been traveling all over the world. I believe I'm singing better than ever before. So I'm very happy for that."

Like Father, Like Son

Enrique has also been very busy, recording, acting, and touring. In 2001, his second English album, *Escape*, was released. Early in

> ### Fun Fact
>
> Julio loves his latest album, in part because he wrote so many of the songs on it. As he noted in *El Mundo* magazine, "I have a very stable sentimental life. *Divorcio* means more [than just an] album in my career. It is more mine than others, because I have written more songs. I can only say that I am satisfied of the result and of [*sic*] having finished it!"

These two photographs feature Enrique Iglesias in Pepsi Cola's 2004 "Dare for More" advertisement campaign. Above: a still from the "Pepsi Gladiators" commercial. Below: the image Pepsi used to introduce their new campaign to the press.

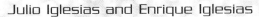

Enrique *(right)* starred alongside Antonio Banderas *(left)*, Johnny Depp, and Salma Hayek in the 2003 film *Once Upon a Time in Mexico*. In the critically acclaimed film, Enrique plays Lorenzo, who is El Mariachi's (or Banderas's) cohort.

2002, he shot a video for the title track with Russian tennis player Anna Kournikova. Reports from the set described a hot romance that took place while the cameras were rolling—as part of the video—and after as well. Soon Enrique and Anna were a couple, a fact that displeased Anna's previous boyfriend, Russian hockey player Sergi Federov. The two had just recently broken up.

Enrique's third album in English, *7*, was released in 2003. He made his acting debut that same year in Robert Rodriguez's *Once Upon a Time in Mexico*, starring Salma Hayek and Antonio Banderas. With his amazing musical success, popular videos, and acting jobs, Enrique should have a career just as long as that of his father's.

TIMELINE

1968   • July: Julio wins the Benidorm Song Contest with "La Vida Sigue Igual" and signs a contract with Columbia Records.

1969   • June: Julio tours Spain.

1970   • July: Julio enters the Eurovision Song Contest with his song "Gwendolyne."

1973   • Julio has sold more than 10 million albums.

1974   • June: Julio releases *A México*, an album recorded in Spanish.

1975   • May: Julio performs a sold-out concert at Madison Square Garden in New York City.

1981   • Julio has sold more than 91 million albums.

          • October: Julio releases *De Niña a Mujer* and poses for the cover photo with his daughter, Chabeli.

1983   • September: Julio receives the first and only Diamond Record Award ever given to a performer by the *Guinness Book of World Records* for selling more records in more languages than any other musical artist in history.

1984   • March: Julio releases his duet with Willie Nelson, "To All the Girls I've Loved Before." It later goes to number 1 on the country charts and number 5 on the Billboard Top 40.

          • August: Julio releases *1100 Bel Air Place*, which eventually goes quadruple platinum, selling more than 4 million copies.

1985   • Julio is awarded a star on Hollywood's Walk of Fame.

1995   • September: Enrique's first single, "Si Tu Te Vas," hits number 1 on the Billboard Hot Latin Tracks chart. It stays at number 1 for eight weeks.

          • December: Enrique's first LP, *Enrique Iglesias*, is released.

1996   • May: *Enrique Iglesias* goes to number 1 on the Billboard Latin Top 50 Albums, where it remains for eleven weeks.

          • June: *Enrique Iglesias* is certified gold.

          • November: *Enrique Iglesias* is certified platinum.

1997   • January: Enrique releases *Vivir*, his second LP.

          • February: Enrique wins a Grammy Award for Best Latin Pop Performance (*Enrique Iglesias*).

          • March: Julio receives the Monaco World Music Award for Best Latin Singer.

1997
- May: *Vivir* is certified platinum.
- September: Julio receives the ASCAP (American Society of Composers, Authors, and Publishers) Pied Piper Award, the society's most prestigious honor for entertainers.

1998
- January: Both Julio and Enrique are nominated for an American Music Award for Favorite Latin Artist. (Julio wins.)
- September: Enrique's third LP, *Cosas del Amor*, is released.
- October: *Cosas del Amor* goes to number 1 on the Billboard Latin Top 50 Albums, where it remains for eight weeks.

1999
- January: *Vivir* is certified gold. Enrique wins an American Music Award for Favorite Latin Artist.
- February: Enrique is nominated for a Grammy Award for Best Latin Pop Performance.
- October: Enrique's single "Bailamos" goes to number 1 on the Top 40 pop charts. It stays there for three weeks.
- November: Enrique releases *Enrique*.

2000
- January: *Enrique* is certified platinum.
- July: Enrique's duet with Whitney Houston, "Could I Have This Kiss Forever?," enters the Top 10.

2001
- January: Enrique wins an American Music Award for Favorite Latin Artist.
- October: Enrique releases *Escape*.
- December: Enrique's single "Hero" goes to number 1 on the pop charts.

2002
- January: *Escape* is certified double platinum. Enrique wins an American Music Award for Favorite Latin Artist.
- June: *Escape* is certified triple platinum.

2003
- January: Enrique wins an American Music Award for Favorite Latin Artist.
- November: Enrique releases *7*.
- December: Julio releases *Divorcio*.

2004
- February: Enrique hits the Top 40 with "Not in Love," a duet with Kelis.

DISCOGRAPHY

Julio Iglesias

1970	• *Yo Canto* (Spanish), *Gwendolyne* (Spanish)
1972	• *Greatest Hits, Julio Iglesias* (Spanish)
1973	• *Un Canto a Galicia* (Spanish), *A Veces Tú a Veces Yo* (Spanish), *Asi Nacemos* (Spanish), *Tu* (Spanish)
1974	• *A Flor de Piel* (Spanish), *A México* (Spanish)
1975	• *Julio Iglesias en Vina del Mar* (Spanish), *Corazón, Corazón* (Spanish), *El Amor* (Spanish)
1976	• *Julio Iglesias en el Olympia* (Spanish)
1977	• *Greatest Hits* (Spanish), *A Mis 33 Years* (Spanish)
1978	• *Soy* (Spanish), *Mi Vida en Canciones* (Spanish), *The 24 Greatest Songs* (English), *Emociones* (Spanish)
1980	• *Sentimentale* (English), *Hey* (Spanish)
1981	• *De Niña a Mujer* (Spanish)
1982	• *Amor, Amor, Amor* (English), *Momentos* (Spanish), *Por una Mujer* (Spanish)
1983	• *Julio International* (Spanish), *Concierto* (Spanish)
1984	• *1100 Bel Air Place* (English)
1985	• *Libra* (Spanish)
1987	• *Un Hombre Solo* (Spanish)
1988	• *Non Stop* (English)
1989	• *Raíces* (Spanish)
1990	• *Starry Night* (English)
1994	• *Crazy* (English)
1995	• *La Carretera* (Spanish)
1996	• *Tango* (Spanish), *La Vida por Delante* (Spanish)
1998	• *La Mia Vita: I Miei Successi* (Italian), *Minha Vida: Grandes Sucessos* (Spanish), *My Life: Greatest Hits* (English)
2000	• *Noche de Cuatro Lunas* (Spanish)
2001	• *Una Donna Può Cambiar la Vita* (Italian), *Ao Meu Brasil* (Spanish)
2003	• *Frontieras, Perfil* (Spanish), *Love Songs* (English), *Divorcio* (Spanish)

DISCOGRAPHY

Enrique Iglesias

- *Enrique Iglesias* (Spanish)
- *Vivir* (Spanish)
- *Cosas del Amor* (Spanish)
- *Enrique* (English)
- *Bailamos* (Spanish), *Best Hits* (Spanish)
- *Escape* (English/Spanish)
- *Quizas* (Spanish)
- *7* (English)

airplay When a radio programmer plays a particular song on the radio.

annulment A legal or religious decision that ends a marriage.

baccarat A card game in which the winner is the player who holds two or three cards totaling closest to nine.

blackjack A card game in which the object of the game is to accumulate cards with a higher count than that of the dealer but not exceeding twenty-one.

charisma Personal magnetism or charm.

demo A musical recording made for the purposes of signing a contract.

duet A piece of music performed by two singers or instrumentalists.

Eurovision Song Contest A very popular contest held annually in Europe for musical acts.

Grammy An American music industry award.

ironic In strong contrast to what was expected.

pediatrician A doctor who specializes in children's medicine.

perfectionist A person who is displeased by anything that does not meet very high standards.

precipice An overhanging or extremely steep mass of rock, such as a crag or the face of a cliff.

slot machine A gambling game in which a player inserts money and pulls a lever in hopes of matching three or more numbers to win.

tumor An abnormal, sometimes cancerous, growth of tissue.

Web Sites

Due to the changing nature of Internet links, the Rosen Publishing Group, Inc., has developed an online list of Web sites related to the subject of this book. This site is updated regularly. Please use this link to access the list:

http://www.rosenlinks.com/fafa/jiei

 **FOR FURTHER READING**

Daly, Marsha. *Julio Iglesias.* New York: St. Martin's Press, 1986.

Furman, Elina, and Leah Furman. *Enrique Iglesias: An Unauthorized Biography.* New York: St. Martin's Press, 2000.

Lockyer, Daphne. *Julio Iglesias: The Unsung Story.* Secaucus, NJ: Birch Lane Press, 1997.

Talmadge, Morgan. *Enrique Iglesias.* Danbury, CT: Children's Press, 2001.

Van Zymet, Cathy Alter. *Enrique Iglesias (Latinos in the Limelight).* Langhorne, PA: Chelsea House Publishers, 2001.

BIBLIOGRAPHY

Boswell, John, and Michael-Anne Johns. *Enrique Iglesias.* Kansas City, MO: Andrews McMeel Publishing, 2000.

Daly, Marsha. *Julio Iglesias.* New York: St. Martin's Press, 1986.

Furman, Elina, and Leah Furman. *Enrique Iglesias: An Unauthorized Biography.* New York: St. Martin's Press, 2000.

Granados, Christina. *Enrique Iglesias: A Real-Life Reader Biography.* Hockessin, DE: Mitchell Lane Publishers, 2000.

Lockyer, Daphne. *Julio Iglesias: The Unsung Story.* Secaucus, NJ: Birch Lane Press, 1997.

Martino, Elizabeth, Rodolfo Cardona, and Francisco Gonzales-Arias. *Julio Iglesias: Hispanics of Achievement.* Langhorne, PA: Chelsea House Publishers, 1994.

INDEX

About the Author

Acton Figueroa is a writer and children's book editor living in New York. He is the author of the *New York Times* best sellers *I Am Spider-Man* and *Spider-Man Saves the Day.*

Photo Credits

Cover (left) © Carlos Alvarez/Getty Images; cover (right) © Deborah Feingold/Getty Images; pp. 1, 4 (inset) © AP World Wide Photos; p. 4, 30 © Getty images; p. 6 © Dennis Barna/Globe Photos, Inc.; p. 7 © Reuters/Corbis; pp. 8, 20, 38 © Globe Photos, Inc.; pp. 14, 30 (inset) © Contifoto/Corbis Sygma; p. 15 © Cardinal Stephane/ Corbis Sygma; pp. 17, 18 © Bettmann/Corbis; p. 23 © Rodriguez Alvaro/Corbis Sygma; p. 27 © Pace Gregory/Corbis Sygma; p. 28 © Frank Micelotta/Image Direct/ Getty Images; p. 29 © Sebastian D'Souza/Getty Images; p. 32 © Scott Gries/Getty Images; p. 34 © Susana Vera/Reuters/Corbis; p. 36 (top) © John Gichigi/Getty Images; p. 36 (bottom) © Photo montage for Pepsi/Getty Images.

Designer: Nelson Sá; **Editor:** Annie Sommers;
Photo Researcher: Nelson Sá